No One Came for Me

By
Indigo Blue

Copyright ©2022 Indigo Norwood

All rights reserved. No part of this book can be duplicated in any form without the written permission of the author and publisher except in the case of brief quotations in book reviews.

ISBN 13: 978-0-9986774-5-3

First Printing April 2022
Printed in the United States of America

I have recreated events, locales, and conversations from my memories of them. To maintain their anonymity in some instances I have changed the names of individuals and places, I may have changed some identifying characteristics and details such as physical properties, occupations, and places of residence.

Testimonial

I know how it feels to not have anyone, and that's why I started my youth program (B.O.M.B) BUNCH OF MIGHTY BELIEVERS. It was geared towards young ladies and its purpose was to show them sisterhood and keep them out of the streets. Like most things, that was just the beginning. Running that program successfully led to my nonprofit organization, "All in One Family Service Network".

Giving back to those in need is important to me with my focus being single mothers.

Back in 2016, I served more than 200-single mothers with essentials and necessities needed to run a household. Another project that I'd started in the basement of my home.

Not having much myself, I started off collecting donations. I would make social media posts where I urged people to donate anything from used baby clothes to toddler and adult clothing. You name it I asked for it! Before I knew it, the organization blew up!

I hadn't expected the city to support me like this. I had a basement full of materials, which led to me getting a small space and turning it into a thrift store. Although my thrift store isn't currently open, I still talk and speak like it is because the trials and tribulations I went through in life led me closer to my real passion.

In the midst of it all, transforming, I received 3 awards for the work I've done in the community. I now own a daycare, and a party event business, that further expresses my belief in the importance of family. Both businesses dealing primarily with families on a regular basis, shows how deep down inside my soul I feel that this is my calling. The universe has shown me many signs.

THIS IS MY TESTIMONY!

I'm not sharing my story for people to feel sorry for me because this right here is what made me who I am today and I'm proud to say it!

When I reflect on my life, I'm glad I went through everything I've been through!

I'm sharing my story hoping someone who is going through something similar, or has been through it, reads this and decides not to give up!

I stayed strong through it all and I never lost faith. The universe always gave me strength and I'm not embarrassed or ashamed of what I've been through.

Here I am!

Standing strong!

Staying humble!

Not forgetting that I have come from nothing, reaching out to others, and helping others who've been through the same or worse.

I am sharing my testimony for young ladies and maybe even young men that may be going through a transition and want to feel comfortable sharing their story!

Breaking your SILENCE!

You may be afraid to talk about your experiences and it's true not everyone is strong enough to get through their situations. Some people just don't know how or even know where to begin. No one will ever know how hard that pain used to hit! Just imagine most of your childhood and teenage years being miserable, sad, and not being able to enjoy being a child.

Simply just wanting to DIE!!!!!

Then you overcome it ALL! Just by keeping FAITH! You can't tell me this doesn't need to be SHARED! I wish I had someone like me growing up that could have shared their story with me.

So! To anybody who's going through it mentally, physically, or just afraid to speak up please don't give up because there is someone who knows your pain and cares!

My testimonial to you if you are going through any type of sexual, physical, and/or emotional and mental abuse, *NEVER GIVE UP!*

LET IT HURT!

LET IT BLEED!

LET IT HEAL!

AND LET IT GO!

It's on you to get you wherever you want to be!

Table Of Contents

TESTIMONIAL 1

A LOOK AT THE WORLD WHEN INDIGO WAS BORN!......... 6

I AM INDIGO NORWOOD.. 8

CHILDHOOD 10

INTRODUCTION 11

FOSTER CARE 13

CHILDREN SERVICES 14

HERE WE GO AGAIN... 17

FOSTER CARE VS FOSTERING A CHILD 23

THE FAST TRACK 37

TRYING TO BE GROWN 38

GRADUATION & GROWN MEN 41

BACK ON BULLSHIT... 45

A ROUGH JOURNEY INTO MOTHERHOOD 50

INDIGO BLUE 54

MRS. UNDERSTOOD 55

TRUE LOVE: ALLINONE 57

SOMETHING FOR YOU! 64

YOUR BEST & WORST 65

CHANGES 70

JUST WRITE! 71

A LOOK AT THE WORLD WHEN INDIGO WAS BORN!

Born Tuesday, December 03, 1991.

In the News In 1991

The U.S. and its allies launch an air attack on Iraq to begin liberating Kuwait. In a ground war that lasts just 100 hours the U.S. led attackers in Operation Desert Storm easily defeat the Iraqi Army. The case against Oliver North is "terminated" with all charges resulting from the Iran-Contra affair dropped. The U.S. Senate approves the Supreme Court nomination of Clarence Thomas, after investigating an allegation of sexual harassment. Brush fire destroys over 3,000 homes and apartments in Oakland, California killing 24 and causing $1.5 billion in damage.

Celebrities born on December 3rd

- Rick Mears, Auto racer-1951
- Katarina Witt, Figure Skater-1965
- Jean Luc Godard, Actor-1930
- Daryl Hannah, Actress-1960
- Ozzy Osbourne, Musician-1946
- Indigo Norwood-1991

Your Zodiac Sign is Sagittarius

The Sagittarius is direct and candid to the point of being blunt. They are philosophical and social endeavors. The Sagittarius is good at seeing the big picture.

Your Birthstone is Turquoise, Zircon

Sports champions in 1991

- MLB- Minnesota Twins
- NFL- New York Giants
- NBA-Chicago Bulls
- NHL-Pittsburg Penguins
- NCAA- BBall- Duke
- KY Derby-Strike the Gold
- U.S. Open Golf- Payne Stewart
- U.S. Open Tennis (Men)-Stefan Edberg
- U.S. Open Tennis (Women)- Monica Seles

Entertainment in 1991

- Nobel Prize Winner-Nadine Gordimer- South Africa
- Best Selling Fiction-Scarlett: The Sequel to Margaret Mitchell's Gone with the Wind, Alexandra Ripley

Best Selling Nonfiction-Me: Stories of My Life, Katharine Hepburn

Best Picture-The Silence of the Lambs-Orion

Best Director- Jonathan Demme, The Silence of the Lambs

Best Actress- Jodi Foster, The Silence of the Lambs

Best Actor- Anthony Hopkins. The Silence of the Lambs

Your Chinese Sign is Sheep

You are sensitive and talented in the arts. If you can stay focused, you

I am Indigo Norwood

It's crazy how life is a revolving door. One misunderstood person can produce several misunderstood people who eventually pedal the continuous cycle of dysfunction. I am Indigo Norwood, the breaker of cycles. I am the voice of the unheard, unwanted, misused, and the misunderstood people of the world!

In fact, that's what I'm going to refer to myself as, Mrs. Understood. I am judged by hypocrites, who are mere wolves in sheep clothing, or at least that's how it seems. Your intense gazes will never reveal what I've been through and it's a blessing. This is my story and my life so, if someone is going to talk about it, let me be the first!

I mean really, who can tell my story better than me?

I'm going to ask that for one minute you remove your lens of worldly views and let me tell my truth.

I am Indigo Norwood born and raised in Akron, OH. I like to think that there once was a time I was carefree and the apple of someone's eye. A cute little bubbly face baby with silky black hair and dimples to die for. I was chunky with fat cheeks and loved on by everyone who was supposed to, correctly.

That was a long time ago and it's augmentable. Something I always struggled with was the thought of birth. Just because you are welcomed into the world, one day in a lifetime, does that mean you are born? Or life begins? For me, I feel as though I was born when I hit the tender age of five. It's the furthest time I can remember back and it's when I feel like my life began. I believe that everyone may have a story to tell but I guarantee mine is worth delving into.

I didn't have it easy and I'm proud to say that I am NOT a product of my past. I like to think of myself as being **resilient**. The capacity to recover quickly from difficulties and toughness is the definition of Indigo.

Psychological resilience is the mere ability to cope with a crisis or to return to pre-crisis status quickly and I exist in knowing that I no longer allow myself to be burdened by the troubles from my past. I am Indigo Norwood, Indigo Blue, the breaker of cycles!

Childhood

child·hood

Part of speech: noun

Definition:

1. The state of being a child

2. The period during which a person is a child

Introduction

Imagine going to bed one night in your comfortable bed, warm sheets after a long day of playing with your big sister only to wake up in a complete stranger's home. As traumatizing as it seems, that's the furthest back I can remember. Indigo Norwood; age five. That's when it seems like life started for me. I began to develop into the person I am today shaped by the choices that others made.

My sister, who I will refer to as Celsey, and I went to sleep on many occasions only to wake up in a different foster home with yet another family. That particular time I was awakened in a set of bunk beds, at some white lady's house with Celsey on top and me on the bottom.

"Don't worry sister, my dad is coming to get us, we won't be here long," Celsey repeated to me several times while holding me tight, very protective. She was all I had because I had no dad to come for me and I was grateful that when her dad came, he would always take us both.

Celsey was very loving and protective when it came down to her little sister and I've always loved her for that. Our relationship and bond strengthened through our life journey. She was always loud, and ghetto and I laugh because she's still the same today. She is very creative, artsy, and loves to cook. And good at it! Her caramel complexion, long hair, and outspoken ways were very different from mine. I was always quiet and timid, and I believe that's what led me to the life I lived.

Back then, I don't remember very much in that time, or how long we stayed there, but her dad came for her, and like always he took us both. My mother, who we are going to refer to as Tarren, wasn't always the most responsible, caring mother that every child desired. She was more for herself, getting caught up in the street life and leaving us to fend for ourselves on many occasions.

I had once been told by Celsey that our mother once was a "bomb" mom before the drugs. She was loving, caring, and took very good care of us. She took us places and treated us very well, spoiling us, something that I don't remember. For me, the negative outweighed the positive regarding Tarren in my eyes. She was never a good mom to me, and I still kind of resent her for that to this present day.

Tarren was a cold hairstylist. She was very pretty with thick, long pretty hair, very sociable and always brought good vibes when she'd enter a room. Her light skin was flawless, and she had long legs even though she was average in height. Beautiful is to say the least when describing her. It's unfortunate that her beauty was skin-deep. She didn't have the confidence that she should have possessed, and it spread like wildfire to the people she should have taken care of and protected. It was surprising because she was raised so far from what she had taken us through.

Tarren's mother, my grandmother, worked at Chrysler and spoiled her and her siblings. It was insinuated that her mother also had a dark side and was very abusive to my mother. She was never given any love or affection, something that she'd reciprocated through us. You'd think that she would've broken the cycle, but it was the total opposite.

Tarren's abusive lifestyle and low self-esteem flourished, leading her down a path of destruction. During this time, she started to hang with my biological father's sister and that's how I was conceived.

*****

Foster Care

A temporary service provided by States for children who cannot live with their families. Children in foster care may live with relatives or with unrelated foster parents. Foster care can also refer to placement settings such as group homes, residential care facilities, emergency shelters, and supervised independent living.

Children Services

Sometimes, kids are placed in homes for long periods of time and other times just for a few days. Children Services first became involved with me and my family as far back as February of 1994. My list of placements and dates are listed below:

First Home:	2/15/94 to 2/16/94
Second Home:	11/14/95 to 11/17/95
Third Home:	11/17/95 to 4/19/96
Fourth Home:	11/14/96 to 11/21/96
Fifth Home:	11/21/96 to 11/3/97
Last Placement:	2/18/02 until Adoption

My first time in a foster home was the result of my mother's drinking and driving. I was taken into the custody of Children Services, and she was placed into a substance abuse treatment program. At that time my mom worked hard to get clean and was doing everything she could to do better as a mom. I was released back into her care under the supervision of my grandmother.

*****

Living with Grandma

My maternal grandmother was a big, pretty woman who everyone loved. She was mixed with Indian and Black and lived in our family house that was passed down to her from her dad who was an Indian. The house was a huge 3-bedroom house with a big garden in the front yard. It received recognition in the Akron Beacon Journal back in the 90's because it was so beautiful. She was also an animal lover who always had a house full of cats and dogs. I don't remember much about living with my grandmother, but I do remember some summer days with her when my mother would drop us off and leave without calling or coming back for days. Grandma would walk me to the McDonald's on West Market Street and buy me Happy Meals.

Being at Grandma's from what I remember was always joyful. I would play with the other little girls around the neighborhood even though I was always different from them and always stood out from the crowd. In fact, most of the little girls in my grandmother's neighborhood didn't like me and I could never figure out why.

Looking back now it was most likely that not everyone liked me because I was a natural-born leader and not easily influenced.

There was this one girl named Ashley who lived in a brick apartment building not too far from where we stayed. She would hang with me despite the other girls' feelings around the way. We played from sunup to sundown and the other little girls would wait for me to go into the house for dinner to play with her because she they could boss her around. She was a follower, and they knew that she'd do whatever they wanted her to do. I wasn't that kid.

Staying with my grandmother during the summer was the best! I knew that with her we were going to be kept clean and fed. She, unlike my mother, was established and at this time wasn't on drugs or drinking or anything like my mother in that sense, at least we didn't see that. She worked for Chrysler and back then people who worked at Chrysler were like Gods. They had money and every year they celebrated their employees by giving them a picnic at Six Flags, which was the largest amusement park in Ohio. Living with Grandma we went there every summer for their company picnic, but life with her in general was always good for me. I learned as an adult some stories my sister tells me about things that was going on when I was a kid, but it was hidden from me.

Celsey told me that my grandmother would get drunk and accuse her of stealing her money and jewelry. Celsey told me that she would rant and rave for hours until she sobered up and apologized to her only to get drunk and do it all over again. I believe her because as an adult I've witnessed it with my own eyes. I am grateful that I was kept in a child's place back then because back then I needed all the love and affection my grandmother gave me. I don't know how I would've reacted knowing she was somewhat abusing the only true shero I had, Celsey and I am sorry that all my love and attention was at her expense.

My grandmother filled the void that my mother left, and I loved her for that. She was the mother that Tarren couldn't be but eventually she would come back and rip us from the only real home we had. For that I despised her. The minute she decided to be a mother she would take us from my grandma, and it would be weeks before we'd see her again.

I was young during this time when we lived with my grandmother because of mom's addiction and her working to complete the drug and parenting classes. My times visiting and attending the Chrysler picnics were different times throughout my life before I was taken away for good.

*****

Here We Go Again

Living back with mom meant we were back living house to house and apartment to apartment. Her depression and drug addiction had gotten much worse and we, Celsey and I, paid the price. If Celsey was gone with her father, I was stuck with whoever mom decided to leave me with for the day or night. I didn't have an active dad, so when Celsey left with hers, I was alone. My father was consumed with his own drug habit to worry about mom or me. So, *no one came for me.*

When we moved on Sherman Street it consisted of just me, my mother, and my sister. At this time, it seemed like my mother was attempting to get her life together and everything felt normal for once. My grandmother bought everything for our apartment and made sure we didn't have anything to worry about. It was a two-bedroom apartment, so my sister and I shared a room with a bunk bed set that my grandmother bought us.

Everything was seemingly normal for once. Celsey made friends and so did I. Our life had finally started to brighten up living with my mother. Unfortunately, this was the first time I was introduced to "everything good doesn't last".

It wasn't long before my mother linked up with the neighbor and they started getting high together. The neighbor also had a daughter who was my age, so we hung out a lot. We didn't really have a choice because our mothers would leave us home alone to go get high. Celsey was getting older, turning into a teenager so she was finding herself. She wanted to be out with her friends and didn't want to be in the house being robbed of her childhood watching after me. On many occasions, she'd leave me to fend for myself. I hardly received any attention, and I became a loner at a young age, staying that way for a long time.

Sometimes my mom would take me with her, and we would ride in the car with different guys. I would be in the back seat while my mom was in the front seat getting high and drunk. It didn't bother me riding with them as long as I was by my mom's side. The things she did with them didn't bother me either. At times the guys we would ride with would either take her back to their spot and they would go in the room while I sat out front. My mom would fuck them for drugs and money.

Deep down inside I believe that she had even let those guys touch me in exchange for money and drugs. I'll never go on record and confirm, but sometimes I have dreams of it happening to me and I believe that it was from that.

I don't remember many birthday parties growing up. If I had any, other than the one my mother had for me on Sherman Street for my 7th birthday, it wasn't much. It was very small and intimate. A few friends from the block, a cake, and some ice cream. I still have a picture from that day of me and my mother holding my birthday cake. It might not have been much, but it meant the world to me.

No matter how many times my mother left me home alone and struggled with her drug addiction, I truly loved and appreciated her and what she tried to do for me while she was sober. She taught me at an early age to be grateful and humble.

As time went on things got worse and my mom's drug and alcohol addiction caused arguments between her and my sister, which led to my sister leaving for good.

A few years passed by, and my mother had given birth to her first son "Mike". The first few years my mother and my brother's father, whose name was also "Mike", were together he was wrapped up in so many illegal things that he eventually ended up turning his name into something else. No one really cared for him and didn't like that my mother was dating him and had a baby with him.

My mother eventually ended up moving out of our apartment and moved us in with Mike's mother, on Welton Street. It was a huge white house that housed many people. In addition to my family, she also had two adopted daughters that were around the same age as me who I eventually bonded with over the years of us saying there.

Mom never dated the same man for too long and it didn't matter if they shared a kid. Mike was into so many things that my mother decided to leave him and moved on with another man that she'd met at one of the Chrysler picnics that my grandmother had taken us to.

Mr. M and my mother started dating when I was about 9-years old, and my brother was four. It's hard to discuss this point in my life because I always believed that maybe if she'd never met Mr. M we would have ever been taken away. Celsey at this point had completely moved out and was living with her dad leaving my brother and me.

We were living in a one-bedroom apartment on Johnston Street in east Akron. My mother's drug addiction had gotten worse and life at home was terrible. The only thing I had to look forward to at this point was the afterschool program I attended at the community center. It wasn't far from Mason Elementary, which was the school I attended.

I loved going there every day after school especially on Fridays. Every Friday we got to watch movies and eat popcorn. But soon all that changed once my brother became old enough to start kindergarten. My life had changed drastically. I would have to walk us both to school every morning, take him to class, and make sure he was okay before I was able to go to my own classroom. I did everything for my little brother at home and at school while my mom either stayed at home sleep or ran the streets.

Her boyfriend was so nice to us most likely because he felt sorry for us. Mom wasn't shit and he knew it. He would work all day and come home and cook for us. He knew our mom was out getting high, neglecting us. When she did decide to take us along, we'd sit there and watch her, and our cousin get high.

I never understood why he put up with my mother's addiction and disrespect for herself and even us kids when he himself wasn't an addict. We would hear them arguing after mom would be gone for days on a binge and he'd threaten to call Children's Services because he was fed up with taking on her responsibilities.

I don't know if my mother took it as a joke, but we'd later find out that he would follow through with his threats and our lives would change forever.

Things between the two of them got worse. My mom was comfortable leaving us for weeks at a time leaving us at home to fend for ourselves. Where Celsey once used to be, having to be the one looking out for me, I now had to look out for my little brother. I would come home to find the house keys in the mailbox, and I knew I'd have to make sure we ate and got baths. I quickly got over the pain of not having mom around and was thankful that at least I had my brother. I wasn't totally alone through this hell.

Mom wasn't there to cook, clean, help with homework, check our homework, or even read a book to us. We had no one. I had gotten so used to taking care of us that it had become routine.

Slowly but surely, Celsey started coming around after months without hearing from her. She came and picked us up on weekends and we would go over to her dad's house, and it would be so much fun. We could be kids again. I had kids my age to play with and I wasn't solely responsible for Mike. When Mike didn't come, I always wondered if mom left him alone or hungry like she'd do if I was there.

At home things continued to get worse and being young I never considered mom's state of health. I knew she was on drugs, but I had no clue what she was battling mentally. The first time she tried to commit suicide I was only three. I didn't know what was going on, but I was older now.

One evening we were at home watching TV and she hopped up and grabbed a knife and put it to her throat. Fear stricken; I didn't know what to do. Could you imagine the fear and pain running through me to witness my mother trying to end her life in front of us? I pleaded with her. Begging her to please put the knife down. My brother was crying and I at 10-years old was trying to talk my mother out of killing herself.

Time moved on and things seemed like they'd never change. Mom's boyfriend was fed up with her shenanigans and tired of raising and solely taking care of kids that weren't his. He felt sorry for us and knew we deserved better. Finally reaching his breaking point he did what he felt was the right thing to do, and our lives changed forever.

It was a late evening and I had done my normal routine. I walked us to and from school and got us some dinner to eat. Mike and I were sitting watching TV in the living room and mom's boyfriend walked in with a children's service caseworker. At this point, it had been well over a week since we'd seen our mom and though my brother didn't know what was going on I did.

He started to explain to me that we could no longer do this. He told me that it was wrong for me to have to take care of my brother and that he could no longer watch us take care of ourselves. He apologized saying it was hurting him to do this, but he had to because how we'd been living was wrong. I felt numb. I had been through this before so I knew that it would be a while before I saw my mom. I knew that we would be taken away, but I never expected the way that it had turned out.

In February 2002, he had made the call and along with the caseworker the police came and removed us from our home. We both were sent to Ms. Sarah until Mike was eventually sent to live with his paternal Grandmother. Even though I had seen Ms. Sarah a few times because she was Celsey's Step Aunt, I didn't know her. She wasn't family. She wasn't Blood. I wanted to be with my family, my mother, my father, my grandmother, but I couldn't. And sadly enough, NO ONE CAME FOR ME.

Foster Care Vs Fostering a Child

I learned the difference between the definition of "foster care" and what it is to "foster a child" very quickly. Fostering a child is the basics of what foster care **really** means. It is a temporary service provided by states for children who cannot live with their families. Children in foster care may live with relatives or with unrelated foster parents. It doesn't say anything about loving that child as if they're your own even if it's only "temporary". It says nothing about protecting them or nurturing them. I was a foster child, a *child* raised by someone who was not my natural or adoptive parent. I was a needy child who needed someone to do what my mother and father couldn't and yet I never received it, correctly.

Pulling up to Channelwood, our new "home" was a three-bedroom apartment. My foster mother "Ms. Sarah" and her boyfriend at the time shared one room, my brother and I shared a room, sleeping on bunk beds and the third room was Ms. Sarah's only biological child, her son, and another male foster child.

Things started off rocky. Ms. Sarah was breaking the rules by letting her felon boyfriend live with her in a state-funded apartment, with foster children. He was creepy with a bald head and big eyes.

Being here had my stomach all twisted in knots, and I could only hope that all this lasted long enough for my mother to get her shit together if not forever, at least long enough to get us back. I mean how hard could it be? All she needed was to find a stable home, drop clean piss, and get into a drug program to get clean. Oh! Let's not forget the easiest requirement of all, make it to every child visitation.

I mean it sounds easy, right?

If you want your kids, prove it! She knew where we were and that we were together, so at least complete the simple requirements to get us back, but for my mother even that was hard.

Time went on and so many children came and went. I watched Ms. Sarah struggle to give them back even through short-lived stays because she'd become attached to the kids while my mother struggled to walk 2-minutes down the street to visit my brother and me as part of one of the "simple" requirements to get us back. Her lack of care was obvious, and I lost hope fast.

I had grown comfortable with disappointments and learned to adapt to new surroundings from when I lived with my mother, so when it started to happen with Ms. Sarah, I was used to it. I had been to so many different schools already from the time I started kindergarten, living house to house, always moving around it didn't even bother me to go to a new school.

I was thankful that I was able to start Leggit in my correct grade, but I felt bad that my brother didn't. He repeated his previous grade level because he wasn't where he should be academically, and it wasn't even his fault. It was a struggle for him because he never stayed in a school long enough to learn, he wasn't being taught at home, and he developed disabilities as a result. My brother suffered from everything, speech impediments, multiple learning disabilities, and ADHD all because of our dysfunctional upbringing. Ms. Sarah couldn't handle my brother and all the things he had going on and grew frustrated with him. I had no idea that she arranged for him to leave and when I found out I was distraught. He was picked up by his father's mother who we once lived with prior to all this happening. She had had several foster children living with her even when we did, but for Indigo it was as it always had been. My siblings had family and I didn't for that reason, just as before, *no one came for me.*

I was left alone and tired of moving place to place therefore my focus was to do my best in school and stay in Ms. Sarah's grace. She was the only good thing in my life in a long time. Grades weren't a problem but the minute I walked into Leggit I heard the whispers.

"She thinks she's cute with those ponytails in her hair like a little girl." They laughed, joked, and made fun of me. They talked about my hair, my clothes and everything Indigo. I had never been bullied so this was new to me. I felt as though I dressed nice, the best I had ever dressed, it wasn't name brands, but I was clean, and I looked nice. I knew what it was to not be liked by girls having that experience when I lived with my grandma but being bullied was different.

Adapting

Adapting to life alone was hard for me. I started this fostering journey with Celsey and when she left, I had my brother, but now he was gone, and I was living life with no real family around me. Holidays were hard and even though Ms. Sarah always went all out for me it didn't fill the void I had inside.

Making friends around the neighborhood was easy once I linked up with a few other foster kids who were like family to me. I met them through Ms. Sarah's son's grandmother. We would run the neighborhood and attend summer camps together at the church. One summer I got into big trouble with Ms. Sarah because one of my friends wrote a nasty letter to a boy who I had a crush on. I tried to tell everyone that it wasn't me, but no one believed me. I was labeled "fast" and at that moment I was looked at differently.

I was already struggling with depression, abandonment, mommy, and daddy issues and whatever else back then at such a young age and now I was looked at in a negative way over something that wasn't even my fault. I hated life and went into a deeper depression barely talking to anyone.

Ms. Sarah's mother was dying, and I was forced to stay at daycare until I was old enough to stay home alone. Social services had stopped attempting the supervised visitations with Tarren because she barely showed up and I had come to the realization that I was never going home. Ms. Sarah's boyfriend left her and had become depressed. Everything happened back-to-back and wasn't letting up. Overwhelmed and crashing fast she decided a change in environment would be good for all of us and that's how we ended up on the westside.

Living on Greenwood surprisingly things were starting to look up for us. I had been with Ms. Sarah for two years at this point and we had a better relationship than I had ever had with my mom. I finally had the stability I needed. We frequently went on vacations, and I was going to the sixth grade at a new school. Ms. Sarah had a new man that moved in with us quickly, but we were happy. It was summertime and I met new friends, a set of twins, who lived next door.

Things were really looking up for me and Ms. Sarah. I had not one, but two best friends and Ms. Sarah had a new boyfriend, named "Allen" from Alabama. She moved him in fast before any of us kids got to meet him.

Truth be told, I always got a weird vibe around Allen, but being an over-thinker, I just wrote it off. I now know as an adult that my reservations came from me knowing he wasn't all the way there mentally. He suffered from bipolar schizophrenia. One day he was cool and the next day he wasn't. He'd be walking around the house talking to the voices in his head.

Beginning my 6th grade year, I attended Perkins middle school, and yet again I was picked on. This time it wasn't about clothes or my hair it was because I didn't come from the same elementary school as most of the kids. I started having problems at home again and school made things worse for me. I had no social life, or friends because I spent most of my time in the house babysitting the other foster kids and it consumed me. My life was school and babysitting. I wanted to run away so bad that I planned it all out.

Ms. Sarah worked a lot and was never home and on her days off she was out partying as if she had forgotten she was a mother. She would leave us kids and Allen at home without any worries. I was completely over it and put my plan into motion. I waited until Ms. Sarah left for work and Allen and the kids were in the house. I walked from Greenwood and Stoner all the way to the mid-rise Spring Hill apartments, where my sister Celsey was staying at the time.

She was surprised to see me and concerned that I had walked all the way there alone and forced me to call Ms. Sarah. I begged her not to make me and told her how bad I needed her. I was lost and confused, and my sister was exactly what I needed. She still made me call Ms. Sarah as if she'd notice I was gone away. I didn't have a mom or a dad I was struggling and needed attention, I needed my sister, at least.

I was forced to go back home, and nothing changed even with me explaining why I didn't what I did. Ms. Sarah was back to work; I was back to babysitting and taking care of the house, spending most of my days with Allen. We started to build what I thought was a father-daughter bond. I had no idea what he had in store for me or that I'd fall in love with him.

Sometimes, I hate to talk about my life during these times because it makes it seem like life was miserable with Ms. Sarah when, she did a lot of stuff with us kids. She spent most of her days working and on weekends kicking it, but during our school breaks she'd spoil us, and we'd travel the world going to different places like Kalahari, New York, Universal Studios, and Disneyland. We even went to China. She was a horrible mother and made up for it with that.

How ironic was life though? I was removed from my mother's care because I was left alone to take care of my younger brother, and I had now been placed in the care of another woman to do that very same thing. Life hadn't gotten all the way better for me and just my luck, returning to Ms. Sarah's after I'd ran away things were only about to get worse.

*****

Molestation

After my short-lived escape things around the house didn't change. When summer arrived, things were better because I didn't have school to worry about and it made things around the house easier. I didn't have to come out my room until Ms. Sarah was gone and that was to look after the kids.

My bedroom was in the basement of the house, and I absolutely loved it. I had my own space, even though it was a basement, it was finished and had three separate rooms. There was a laundry room, a TV room with a bar and barstools, and my bedroom that was purple and pink. I had a pet parrot that talked all the time and the only thing that I didn't have was a TV, I had one of those old rotary telephones. I loved it. It was mine. For the most part, no one ever came into my room, and I loved that too. It wasn't until one summer night I was awakened out of my slumber to someone kissing and touching me all over.

It was about three in the morning and the pungent smell of a freshly smoked cigarette invaded my nostrils. Before I could react to the unwanted touching, he entered me whispering, "just relax" softly into my ear. I was surprised when I finally opened my eyes to see Allen on top of me and I hurriedly squeezed them shut. At the tender age of 12, I was losing my innocence to a grown ass man. It didn't last as long as the scars it left on my life forever, it was actually very quick. Within a matter of minutes, Allen had sexed me and was back upstairs and outside smoking another cigarette as if nothing had happened. This was the beginning of what shaped me for the rest of my life.

The rest of the night I kept my eyes focused on the door. I couldn't wrap my mind around what had happened to me. The next morning, I went up for breakfast and everyone around me seemed to be staring at me like they knew what had happened. It really wasn't like that but that's what I felt. Rubbing my leg under the table Allen smiled at me and when everyone cleared out, he grabbed my arm softly and asked me if I enjoyed it.

Did I enjoy it?

I felt so awkward from the question and the nerve of him I softly pulled away from him and went about my normal activities. I didn't answer him because I didn't know how to. Did I enjoy it?

That one night became all my nights living with Allen in the house. Allen would come into my room every single night, and have his way, then smoke a cigarette and go lay-up with Ms. Sarah as if nothing happened. The more Ms. Sarah worked and partied the more Allen had his way with me. Taking advantage of me and the situation, Allen left me used and confused. I never told her because I was afraid, she wouldn't believe me. I mean it was like she never believed anything I said.

Eventually, I grew to enjoy sex with him, and I loved that it was our "little secret". Allen and I had gotten comfortable fast with our relationship. I was having sex with him like I was a grown ass woman. Outside of him fingering me on a ride at Kings Island and him blowing me kisses and winking his eyes at me across the dinner table, we would never have sex anywhere else other than the basement. But we would fuck all over the basement. In the laundry room on top of the washer and dryer, he would eat my pussy and we'd fuck like rabbits. I was happy that he never made me reciprocate that act on him.

I became more attached to Allen and he to me. We would do everything together. While the other kids were at summer camp, we'd fuck and after we'd ride around listening to Pretty Ricky and he'd hold my hand and sing the songs to me. He was always very overprotective of me especially when it came to the other boys in the neighborhood. He wanted me all to himself and I loved the attention he gave me, so I was okay with it.

I craved a man's touch and love, something that I'd never had. I had never had a real male figure in my life until him other than my brother's dad and it wasn't much. I wasn't privy to his sickness, so I didn't understand that he was manipulating me.

One day we were chilling watching a movie and Ms. Sarah walked in and said, "Y'all are a little too close." It never went past that. She was a heavy sleeper and her nights at Summa Hospital kept her ignorant of our relationship. I kept our relationship secret only telling two people I trusted.

One girl I told held our secret for months and that made me feel like what was happening was okay until I told my twin best friends who made me realize that it wasn't. In fact, it was terribly wrong.

I remember the day it all hit the fan. The twin brother had always had a crush on me and was upset when I told him about Allen. I remember that he fussed saying, "That's why I always hated him. This whole time he didn't want us to be friends because he was up in there raping you!" Later that day, the twins' mom told Ms. Sarah and I was interrogated for hours about our "relationship". The secret was out. Something that had been happening for two years right under her nose and she was fed up with it. Although, she still didn't fully believe me until he confessed. She thought I was saying it for attention.

Ms. Sarah offered to take me to the police, but in all reality, she manipulated me against it. She used me being shy and innocent against me saying that we would be in the News and that everyone would know about Allen and me. I didn't want that. Besides the fact that I knew it was wrong, it didn't change that I was in love with him. Despite his wrongs.

As an adult, I don't believe her intentions were to ever take me to the police. She'd also proved that she wouldn't leave Allen either. I feel that she knew what had been going on the entire time and didn't care. She wanted it to happen to me because it had happened to her as a kid. In a way, I feel like she used me to keep him and if it wouldn't have ever come out, we would have been fucking for many more years to come.

Nevertheless, Allen had confessed to everyone about what he'd done, and everyone, but Ms. Sarah, seemed to be bothered by it. He had even suggested that she had "forced" him to have sex with me. Using his mental illnesses as an excuse she continued to date him despite the rumors of her involvement.

She rubbed it in my face that she didn't care about what he had done to me, I mean why should she? I wasn't her "real" daughter. She would blatantly pull up to his apartment and drop him off food. It was like she was trying to prove that he was still her man and not mine. Almost like she won him as if we were two girls or grown women fighting over a man. She continuously made excuses for him raping me. I had had enough and went into a deep depression. She noticed but continued to badger me with their relationship. She didn't put me into counseling or never even asked about how I was feeling or seemed concerned about it all. To me it was like she put it all to the back of her mind and didn't care about what had gone down.

Every day I prayed asking God to send my mom back to me. "Lord just please help her get better and come for me," but she never did.

No one came for me.

All I ever wanted was to reunite with my mom, my sister, and my brother, but it never happened. Time went on and I not only became a prisoner in my house, but I had become a prisoner in my own mind. I was depressed, and sad to say that the only good thing to look forward to at Ms. Sarah's house was my nightly escapades with Allen and now he was gone. And as messed up as it sounds, he loved me or at least made me feel loved. A love that I'd never experienced.

Breaking... Bad

I might have hated my life but there was nothing I could do about it. Still being treated like an in-house babysitter and maid, and the mother of the other children when Ms. Sarah was gone, Cinderella ain't have shit on me! I was the oldest and only still there was because of the ties Ms. Sarah had with Celsey's daddy.

Her son hated me and was always in competition with me. He ruled the house, cussing Ms. Sarah out whenever he wanted to and being a terror to anyone who he felt got in his way it was horrible living with him. He hated that he couldn't control me like he did the other foster kids. All of the foster kids were afraid of him. He would tease them about not having any parents or a real family. He would make them feel so low. I would often take up for them feeling so bad for them. They were so many years younger than us.

To me, it was bad enough they were in a foster home with complete strangers, but to be bullied on top of all of that was straight up awful. Knowing the pain of being raised in foster care and being taken away from what you know, I would pray for them. I prayed that they would be returned home to their mothers' as much as I prayed for Ms. Sarah to discipline her son for his actions, she never did. He had so much hate inside of him it was scary.

I understand now that him going from being an only child to having so many different kids come and go at a young age had to be tough on him. Ms. Sarah didn't pay any of us any attention, he was traumatized just like us. It doesn't, however, excuse the fact that he was a little terrorist. We all were going through a lot, and I can really say that when Ms. Sarah's boyfriend number three showed up it all changed.

"Eric" entered our lives bringing along five kids and a whirlwind of issues. It was like Ms. Sarah was so pressed and so desperate for a man she didn't care what she had to put up with or what they'd do to us. Apart from the issues he'd come with, Eric brought happiness into a place where it had disappeared long before. He kept us all in check and gave us all equal and appropriate love. Her son and him would often bump heads but for me, he was heaven sent. He understood my hurt and pain. He was there for me way more than Ms. Sarah ever had been when it came to my molestation.

You'd think Ms. Sarah would have been an advocate for me since she had experienced the same thing as a child, but she hadn't. She was jealous of our relationship because Eric and I were so tight. He was a good father figure even while fighting with his own demons. As a drug user and an alcoholic, he still had my back when everyone else fought so hard against me.

He defended me against Ms. Sarah all the time when it came to babysitting or always being the one to have to clean up. He was there for my first day of high school, homecomings, and would talk to me about boys. He listened to me about my depression and made it a priority to support me through everything. He was truly like the father I'd never had. He was what I had always wanted and craved for and after living with Ms. Sarah for four years, always being sad and depressed, I was happy for once in my life.

Ms. Sarah and Eric would fight all the time and she'd put him out of our house. Each and every time I'd be dejected, praying he wouldn't stay gone for long. Have you ever experienced losing the one and only thing that keeps you grounded? That was Eric for me. He kept me leveled when everyone else disregarded me. He was my peace and happiness inside of an imperfect home that everyone thought was perfect.

My adoption day came, and I remember it like it was yesterday. Social services came offering me two options. I could stay with Ms. Sarah in a home that had been my home for more than four years. A place that they knew as my safe haven, and me as my hell hole, or I could be shipped off to a group home until another family came and adopted me, which was rare.

In the system kids over the age of 12 make up less than 10% of total kids adopted each year. They have the lowest chance at getting adopted. No one ever wanted the older kids. Hell, Ms. Sarah didn't, she had me by default. Before leaving the house, my sister pulled up screaming and hollering that she didn't want me to be adopted out.

"It ain't right!" Celsey screamed and cried.

"You're full of shit!" Ms. Sarah screamed back. To the fresh eye, Celsey was a loving sister who was putting up a fight to keep her family together, but to Ms. Sarah and me, she was putting on a good act. Ms. Sarah had never done the things that they accused her of claiming she had brainwashed me. Ms. Sarah never kept my biological family away from me. She always gave them the option to see me, spend time with me, and more. They decided to be more worried about themselves than the one person who couldn't take care of herself, me. My mother, father, sister, and grandparents were either strung out on dope, prostituting or just straight up worried about nobody but themselves. They had the option to come and get me, but *no one came for me*.

Now adopted, living with Ms. Sarah, her son, and Eric they were my family. As much as I wanted to go home, I accepted that I never would and lived with it. My years went fast, and I was growing up faster than most girls my age. I had experienced sex at the hands of a grown man, so I was grown. And now that I had an ass and tits there wasn't anything anyone could do to stop me. By fourteen I was fuckin' and my relationships with Eric and Ms. Sarah had become exasperating and completely dissipated.

Even with the adoption final Ms. Sarah didn't give two fucks about me. She would take me over to my boyfriend's house knowing what I was going to do. She'd turn around and become the authoritarian barking orders at me when it was beneficial to her but for me, Eric and her rules went in one ear and out the other. I was done with following everyone else's rules and tired of never being able to make my own decisions. So, after one night of constant bickering, I called up my aunt, my daddy's sister, packed all my stuff, and dipped out months before my 18th birthday.

Although I didn't stay there long, I had moved out of Ms. Sarah's and in with my aunt and favorite cousin in April Court. I had officially entered my wild and free-spirited stage of life. Free to live. Free to be who I desired to be. I left because at the age of seventeen, after years of suffering through depression, molestation, and mental and emotional abuse, *no one came for me.*

This is a picture of Indigo (Right), Ms. "Sarah" (Middle) and (Adoptive Brother) on my adoption day.

The Fast Track

These were my free-spirited years. I spent a lot of time finding myself and that was difficult. I acted out. I sexually exploited myself. I wasn't who I really wanted to be. I did what I felt like I had to do to survive. I was living the fast track, all gas, no breaks!

Trying to be Grown

Once I left Ms. Sarah, my senior year was one for the books. I started missing school from being hungover. I didn't care because I was finally free. Ms. Sarah was still my guardian, so every time I missed school, they would notify her. She would then call me and tell me how I wasn't going to graduate. She would belittle me by telling me I was going to be a dropout, whatever she said didn't faze me. It would go in one ear and out the other. One thing I did know was that I was going to finish school if it was the last thing I would do, just to prove her wrong.

The closer I came to becoming an adult the more she prayed for my downfall. Everything that she said to me was negative and it infuriated her that she couldn't control my life like she wanted to. She wanted me to need her. She wanted me to fail without her. I wasn't though; and even though I grew wilder by the minute, having sex with whoever I wanted to when I wanted to, I was going to be okay.

I had started having real sex. I was grown or trying to be, so I would only fuck grown men. I didn't like boys my age. They did nothing for me. I was 17-years old sleeping with men that were 10-times my senior and would only date men that were 2-to-3 years older. I had been having sex with a grown man since my cherry got popped, what was I going to do with a kid my age?

When I met my first real boyfriend, I didn't even have a type. I liked him because he liked me. I was walking to the bus stop, and he pulled up on me. I thought I was cute, and he thought I was too because by the end of the night we were linking up and shortly after I was his. "Zack" was attractive, but he wasn't gorgeous. He was light-skinned, short, and skinny. I can't even really say how attracted to him I was because honestly, everything started off good and age didn't matter to him. He was 24-years old, and he loved me like I had never been loved and that was good enough for me.

Things started off fast with Zack and because I was living with Celsey now it made it that much easier. In Celsey's and my first apartment together on Fess Street she worked what seemed like 24/7, I was still in high school, so Zack practically moved in. There on Fess Street it was me, Zack, Celsey and her boyfriend. I would go to school when I could during the day and Zack was turning me up by night. He introduced me to all the Valley and Hill niggas. I spent most of my life sheltered, raising other people's kids, and securing other people's checks, so this life was new to me. Zack took me out and showed me off, I loved it.

I was finally doing what other girls my age had been doing. Loving the attention, I was getting, I had a nigga on each side of town, but when I had intercourse with them, I was using protection. I was lived free, but I still believed in being safe. Impressed by the cars and money I was knee deep in doing whatever I could to please them to get whatever my desires were at the time.

I was so ready to graduate, you couldn't tell me anything. I was a birdie with wide wings, spreading them far to fly. I was so invested in myself that I put my relationship with Zack to the test often.

I believe when I met my "Sugar" it had to be the worst. My relationship with him was like no other. Again, I was headed to school at the bus stop, this time in the middle of a blizzard, and he pulled up on me. Seeing this man surprised me because I didn't know what his intentions were for me. "Sugar" rolled down his window and asked if I needed a ride. Now mind you this man is old enough to be my daddy but fine enough to make me moisten in a place that dripped. He was so fine I hopped my young ass right in the car and it was on. I didn't care that he had kids my age and older and

I didn't care that he was old enough to be my father. I wanted him and he wanted me.

Sugar lived ironically across the street from me and Celsey on Fess in an apartment building he owned. I started messing with him tough. Our relationship was mostly me giving him sex and him giving me money. He would take me and pick me up from school and every time we would fuck, and he'd give me money. I thought I was doing something back then. I saw how easy it was to fuck him and get some money it became my little hustle.

Graduation & Grown Men

Prom time was nothing like I'd expected or had even planned for. Maybe a week or two before the actual date I found out I was knocked up. I went to the doctor for stomach pains only to find out I was six weeks pregnant. At this time, I was having unprotected sex all the time and I had never considered this. I was sleeping with both my Sugars, a nickname I had given them, but I never considered this. I was pregnant and in so much pain, which turned out to be an ectopic pregnancy.

An **ectopic** pregnancy is when the baby is formed in your fallopian tubes.

Naturally, I miscarried. I ended up telling each person I was having sex with at the time that I was pregnant and still none of them knew about each other.

Finally, the time had arrived for me to graduate, and Zack gave me a big block party at our spot to celebrate. Everyone I knew was there, and it was completely off the hook. In June 2010, I walked the stage proving everyone who doubted me wrong, defeating all the odds that were placed against me and I was happy and grateful for that. I was in a happy place, and I prayed that it stayed that way. Tarren even showed up to my graduation ceremony, which had always been my dream, and even though she and Ms. Sarah didn't say anything to each other I was grateful.

My mother wanted to be back in my life, and I was all for it. It was something that I'd always dreamed of and had finally gotten. Shortly after I graduated my mom, and her boyfriend at the time moved in with Celsey and me and our men. This was a very small apartment, but we made it work so we could be together. Life for me was finally looking up. I had a family, my family. Unfortunately, like always, me and my family didn't mix. Mom hadn't changed and living with her, and her addiction was a struggle.

Our relationship didn't progress, but since I had graduated, and I was working making my own money I didn't allow it to affect me. I was finally living my life for me. Zack and I were doing good for the most part until one summer day not too soon after I graduated. I was chilling at his homeboy's mother's house with his friend, and he blew down catching me red-handed. I had never played with fire and fucking someone so close to him but that day I felt bold, and it didn't end well for me. It started a life of physical abuse from Zack.

He walked into the basement and me and ole' boy was just chilling. We weren't laid up or anything, but Zack didn't care. He felt disrespected so there, right there in that basement with his friend standing watching he beat my ass like a nigga on the street. I had no help. Down on the ground, Zack started to kick me in the face with his polo boots, punching me nonstop. His feet continuously crashed into my stomach while he screamed, "you down here fucking my nigga huh?!"

I really had no intentions of sleeping with his friend and I know that it may have not been a good look for me to be chilling late at night with his friend in a basement now, but I didn't deserve that. I didn't deserve the continued beatings after. I was a baby still learning how to be a woman. So even though his homeboy knew how it looked and Zack did, I really was that naïve.

The next morning came quickly, and I wasn't prepared for the image I'd seen when I woke up. My face was so badly swollen that I couldn't even recognize myself. This was my first time ever being hit by a man. This changed me. Not in the way you would expect but it did change my feelings toward him. I didn't trust him and now I was completely turned off. This situation also started a lot of stuff with his other friend, Elijah.

Elijah would come over to the house when I was alone and dog Zack out. He would tell me how I deserved better and that turned into him calling me when he would drop Zack off with other girls. He would call me and tell me how Zack was cheating on me. I knew that it was his way of distancing me and Zack because he wanted what he had, but I wasn't feeling that.

One night he pulled up on me after he'd dropped Zack off with another girl. My window was low enough for you to walk up on it and see everything inside, so he tapped on the window. I peeked out and was surprised when I saw Elijah standing there. He gave me a complete rundown about Zack, all his cheating, and how he'd just dropped him off with a girl not even an hour ago. I wasn't feeling any of this anymore and I grew tired. I was tired of being an adult and I started to miss being at Ms. Sarah's. I got rid of his ass and I started to become depressed again and I stayed in my room most days.

I was alone and sad. My mother had been kicked out, and so had Zack. Celsey worked so much that I had no one, but one person and, that was my sister's boyfriend. Here I was once again I was laying in the bed minding my own business and I was woken up to him touching me all over my body. I jumped up and told him to get off me, but it fell on deaf ears. For minutes he tried to force himself on me and I panicked. I didn't know if I was strong enough to fight him like I wasn't strong enough to fight Allen. I didn't want this, and I couldn't believe it was happening again. What is wrong with me that made people think it was okay to do this to me? I battled with thoughts of a sexual aura I had in the atmosphere around me that screamed "**RAPE ME!**" Why did everyone want to hurt me, sexually? So, at that moment I decided that I wasn't that little 12-year-old girl anymore and I yelped as loud as I could muster up for him to get the fuck off me!

He scurried off and I called my foster father to come and get me. I was scared to death waiting for my father to arrive. Livid, he burst through the doors and onto my sister's boyfriend. He wasn't so tough when my dad got there. It was so much going on from my dad screaming for me to pack my shit and him chasing after her boyfriend I couldn't keep up. So, after I got my stuff and left with my dad, I called Celsey to tell her what had just happened. She was my sister, and I knew she loved me with everything she had to give.

I didn't expect what had happened next. When I told her what happened and that I wanted to file a police report she cut me off and told me that she didn't believe me. That night I moved back with Ms. Sarah and my dad. Ms. Sarah was right. She had told me numerous times that Celsey didn't give a fuck about me, and she wasn't down for me, and she was right. I was finally seeing it with my own eyes.

About six months later it came out that he'd tried to touch our 16-year-old little sister, and he ended up doing jail time for sleeping with a 13-year-old girl. It wasn't until then that Celsey finally left him.

Back On Bullshit

Time with my parents didn't last too long. I had gotten a taste of what it felt like to be an adult, I was an adult and I wanted to live like one. I eventually moved out and in with my best friend, Ryder. Ryder and I met years before in one of those brief foster home stays and clicked. Our stories were similar, she had a fucked up, drugged out mother, absent father and no one had come for her either. I was older than Ryder, not by too much, but she was faster than me. She taught me a lot of things that I had never thought about doing like how to boost clothes.

Life with Ryder and her aunt was exciting. It was a party every night filled with liquor and niggas just how I loved it. One night in particular her aunt gave us a small kickback at her house, and we invited all the hood niggas from both the hill and the valley. The party was wild, and I ended up bumping into Zack's friend Elijah's little sister, and I could tell that she was feeling me.

We had a few occasions before where we bumped into each other, and I felt her vibe. She was always the life of the party and I loved to party, but this night was different. This night I was feeling her too and one thing led to another, and we went up to the bathroom and finally tasted each other. When I say "finally" it was just that. We had been around each other so many times, flirting and showing that we wanted each other but that night it went down!

This wasn't my first time with a girl, but this night was different. This night was freaky and lit and eating her pussy and her eating mine was the tip of the iceberg. I always knew I liked girls. This wasn't my first time, so I knew what I was doing, and I showed her how good I was at it. When we finished, I went downstairs grinning from ear to ear. I know it was all over my face what had taken place and Ryder let me know she knew exactly what had happened with quick accusing eyes. What I wasn't expecting was what happened next that changed my life forever. This is where the story gets interesting! This is what I meant when I said it was the tip of the iceberg. I want to say now that I am thankful where my life is now and for the experiences, I've had but I have learned, and I've grown, and I am a better woman today!

Moving on and back to where I left off. I sauntered downstairs, grinning from ear-to-ear after just having the time of my life getting some head from a beautiful bitch and I sat down on the couch and here comes Elijah in my ear. Yup! Her big brother was now in my ear wanting the very thing his sister just had a scoop of and I was all for it. He knew what had just happened, everyone did so why should I care? Now had I known that I would fall in love with him I would've never let any of that happen. Ryder was the main reason I even let it happen. She was in one ear and he in the other. Neither of them wanted me to ever go back to Zack.

"Girl wasn't you just upstairs with his little sister, you off the chains!" Ryder's aunt laughed after she had overheard us talking.

She couldn't be more right. I was off the chains, and she had no idea how far off I'd end up. I didn't even know. What I did know and feel deeply about at that time was I was a big girl. I had been making grown women decisions way before I was supposed to and this was no different, so despite my reservations about moving forward with Elijah because of what had gone down between his sister and me and his ties with Zack, I gave him a shot anyway. It fucked up things with his sister and me, but I didn't care. I always loved dick a little more so when she gave me the ultimatum, I chose him. We were still cool, but we couldn't have sex anymore.

My life was hectic, and I was unsure of myself most of the time. I tested the waters of stripping but that didn't last even a week. I had started to learn a little more about myself and what I liked, and I started to learn how to make real money. So, during my days hanging in the streets, the few stripping days, and going to bars I built a different clientele. One that I had always had with my old men, but I took a different leap and started prostituting with men that I didn't know.

What started with just my two old men sexing them for money turned into a business. Niggas wanted to fuck, and I wanted money. I was straight up. I'd let them know from the beginning what it was so there wouldn't be any misunderstandings.

"If you want to fuck, I want to get paid!"

I remained living with Ryder while I waited for my apartment in Spring Hill, and I made my money by using what I had. My price depended on the client and what they wanted to do. When I got my apartment, it really took off. I didn't have to fuck in cars or go to rooms. They'd pull up and we'd fuck, and they'd be gone. Nobody wanted to live in Spring Hill, but I didn't care. It was stepping a stone for me, and it helped me get exactly where I needed to be.

I was working a real job and running my business right up under Elijah's nose. I would lie to him saying I was working extra hours and I was just not at the job he knew about. I would work all day and party all night, so my apartment had become the spot. I had linked up with one of my homeboys from school and ended up telling him about my prostituting. I trusted him and knew that he wouldn't judge me. Unfortunately, I was wrong yet again.

He talked me into riding up to Cleveland with him to link with one of his boys and I was down for it. He had piped it up saying how much money he had, and how cool he was so I trusted every word this man said to me. He was originally from there so what could go wrong?

We pulled up and he hopped out talking to old dude about what we'd discussed. Sitting in the car I started to get an eerie feeling and cracked my window to see what exactly was going on.

"I ain't paying that hoe. I'ma fuck her and dump her off!" dude said with the straightest face I'd ever seen. I knew this wasn't like any time before and I should've run, but where was I going to go? I was 45-minutes from my city and didn't know anyone here. My friend jumped back in the car like nothing happened not knowing that I heard everything that was said.

"You ready?" he asked, and it scared me that he'd even allow this to happen. We were supposed to be closer than that.

"I ain't feeling this please just take me home," I begged upon deaf ears.

"You trippin', he legit and ain't gon' do nothing to you."

"I'm cool, can you tell him let's link another time?"

"You're going in there now you trippin'"

Against my better judgment, I hopped out and followed him into the house. The closer I got to inside the more my insides turned. I stopped in my tracks and told dude that I wasn't feeling it. He didn't care. He lunged at me and tried to snatch me all the way in the house. I took off running away from the door and towards the car. My friend pulled off leaving me so, I just ran down the street and continued to run until I found a public place. Catching a cab home, I never heard from that friend again and I was happy. You would think any logical and sane person would turn their life around and find a better way to make money after I was going to be drugged, raped, and possibly killed but it didn't. It was too easy to lay on my back and get fucked for a couple hundred. The money was fast. It didn't take much to lay, let him nut, and I got paid just like that.

It was the life. I had a pretty good gig going and I loved it. My lifestyle was fast, and I enjoyed it. Like most good things, they always come to an end. For me, it wasn't any different. I woke up one morning feeling sick to my stomach. Ryder, Elijah's sister, and I were chilling, and I told them I thought I was pregnant. That same day I took a test, and it came back positive. That wasn't good enough for me. I needed real proof that my life that had just got started was about to be over just like that. So, I made an appointment and a short time after the doctor confirmed. I didn't go back and tell the girls I just kept it to myself. It wasn't hard because I was always a private person. Thinking about the baby but not quite ready to give up on everything I had built, I lessened my client load and started to just focus back on my two old men.

When I finally shared the news with Elijah, he was happy and wanted a girl from the start. We were enjoying our pregnancy until his messy mom and friends started a rumor that it was Zack's. Now I hadn't been with Zack in years, so why would they put them papers on me? I didn't know. I had never been with those two at the same time. My life had been changing drastically and all I could do was prepare to be a mom and I wasn't letting anyone interfere with that.

A Rough Journey into Motherhood

Getting pregnant slowed me down a lot, but I kept Sugar #1 around. He was convenient for me. I had been messing with him so long I was as comfortable with him as I was Elijah. I had never really been attracted to any of my tricks, I didn't like or love any of them including him, it was just business. Besides he already had anywhere between 25-30 kids and 15-20 baby mothers. He meant nothing to me outside of our routine, one that eventually led him into becoming infatuated with me. He was totally in love with me and wouldn't allow me to leave him alone, even if I wanted to.

He would pick me up every morning from my apartment. When Elijah was home, I'd have him park at the bottom of the hill and I'd walk down. Giving me rides to-and-from work we would stop at his house and have sex. In exchange, he would either give me money or it'd be to pay my debt for rides. This lasted up until I was six months pregnant. I had tried to leave him alone many times before, but I needed the money and the rides. Elijah didn't have a car and neither did I and I was never going to step foot on a bus. I had never before, and I wasn't then. So, I kept him around up until my belly started to show.

Banned from Spring Hill Elijah was no help when our daughter finally arrived. A new mom too scared to be alone I spent most of my time staying back with Ms. Sarah and my foster dad. That only lasted so long because I was a new mom and wanted to be a family with Elijah. So, we copped our first house on the east side on McKinley Street. Our daughter was only one and that Christmas he proposed to me. I had finally gotten the one thing I had never had in my life, a family, one that had the same blood as me.

I had never had a real family so this was new to me and unfortunately, I didn't know what to do with it. I had my baby and my family, but I also had my tricks blowing my phone up wanting this good thang back, and I spiraled back into my old lifestyle. I tried to keep from falling but at the end of the day I needed them just as badly. As long as they knew I needed them, they had the upper hand. Sugar #2 had missed me, and his needs and desires had changed during our short time apart. He had a new infatuation with threesomes, and I was all for it. I liked pussy so this was nothing for me. I put my homegirls on and that led to me and him having threesomes with my childhood friends. Just like my first time sleeping with Twin back in the day, I put her on to my Sugar. It wasn't anything that she wasn't into anyway we just got to be together again.

I wasn't only having sex with girls because I was making good money and he wanted me too, I was into them. I don't know if my love for women came from the abuse I'd suffered as a young girl or if I was living in a time where being who you wanted to be and being with who you wanted to be with wasn't so traditional anymore. I never thought too deep in it. All I knew was I enjoyed being with a bad bitch or two every now and then.

It seemed like it was the new norm for me. I was tricking with my Sugar having threesomes and then it turned into threesomes for my own pleasure for fun. Things with Elijah weren't quite working out. I needed some excitement in my life, and he wasn't it at the time. It was New Year's Eve, and I was out having the time of my life. It was lit and I was partying with my best friends going hard. "Princess" and I were always close, so I never expected what happened that night to happen. It had gotten late but the party was still going, and Princess started flirting with me. One thing led to another, and we started kissing and she confessed that she'd had a crush on me. It was unexpected but I was with it and of course we ended up in the bedroom. Her baby dad came in and we all three had some fun.

It was crazy because we were in the back room having a full-out, freaky threesome while the party was still rocking. It had a good number of people out there so it is still to my surprise that Elijah would pull up and catch us red-handed. We were all fumbling trying to get dressed all while he was honking the horn and then beating on the door. As hard as we tried to play, he wasn't a fool. He knew exactly what we were doing and because of that, I had to give him one.

I didn't really care because he was my man and I loved him despite our differences at that time. It didn't help because things with him were still shaky. Summertime hit and I started going out with Princess. We were very close and did everything together at that point. We were out one day, and I met a guy named Austin.

Austin started out as a good dude. We hung out a lot doing just about any-and-everything together. I was really into him until things changed. What started out as a good friendship had drastically changed the minute, he found out Elijah was my baby's father. They were archenemies. I had no idea of this and didn't find out until Austin and I were locked in for life. As a woman thinking back now, I know that I wasn't anything but a pawn in the game he wanted to play with Elijah, and it worked.

It seemed like everyone knew about their little beef but me. Elijah's mom knew the entire time about Austin and my relationship and never once mentioned that they were beefing with each other. She would be in the car with me when I pulled up on Austin or would drop me off to him. She knew the entire time, now that was some low-down scandalous shit. I should've known she couldn't be trusted I mean she was my baby's dad mom taking me and riding with me knowing I'm cheating on her son but at the time I wasn't thinking. It was nothing to me. Unfortunately, I didn't find out until I was pregnant with his baby, but it reminded me of a hard lesson, and that was I couldn't trust anyone. I had always been by myself; this wasn't any different.

I was pregnant and an abortion was the last thing on my mind. Yeah, my situation wasn't ideal but even if it meant I had to raise this baby alone killing it wasn't an option. Breaking the news to Austin was cool until outside people tried to accuse me of messing with Elijah after I had officially let everyone know Austin and I were together. It was true but that did not mean I didn't know who fathered my baby. When his cousin started telling him about me still messing with Elijah, Austin changed. He gave me an ultimatum, either leave and move to Columbus with him leaving my daughter and everyone behind or get rid of the baby. I wasn't comfortable with that. I had been left by my own mother and no one came for me. I could never have given my daughter that same fate. After that everything really went downhill until we eventually split.

I was left pregnant again and didn't know what to do. In that moment I did what I felt was best. I know now as an adult that the decision I made next wasn't the best but, in the end, it still worked out for my kids. Knowing Elijah was still in love with me I ran to him and told him the baby was his.

INDIGO BLUE

I am Indigo Blue. I have taken a chance on me and on life. I have taken the time to reinvent who I want to be. I am Indigo Blue, the breaker of chains. I am a mother, a daughter, a granddaughter, and a sister. I am a CEO, an entrepreneur, a mom, a boss, I Am Indigo Blue a SURVIVOR!

Mrs. Understood

I like to think of myself as Mrs. Understood. I am married to the fact that people will probably never understand why I did what I did, and I am okay with that. People have taken it upon themselves to judge me and consider me a hoe because of my lifestyle. They assume I did it for pleasure, but for me, it was about the money. It was always about the money. I have learned throughout my years that I am bisexual. I love who I love and like who I like and grant it, one of my main attractions are older men and the love and attention they give me.

I have always loved the attentiveness older guys gave. Fucking any man between the ages of 40-50 years old I was always getting money and it was a high reward. I'm not sure where the label "hoe" stemmed from but like most other things I chose to not let it define me. Calling me a hoe never bothered me. Those men I was being a "hoe" for were the ones taking care of me and looking out for me when everyone else left me high and dry. I was a mother of one and had one on the way.

The day that I had my son was way more emotional for me. I had been cut off from his biological father and I had convinced his enemy that it was his baby as a result. It wasn't until days after he was born that I had enough courage to tell Elijah the baby wasn't his. I didn't have a choice because Austin's cousin who had been playing the middleman between all of us had already told Elijah whose baby man son really was, and it broke my heart for him to find out like that. Knowing that Elijah wasn't my son's dad had literally eaten me alive my entire pregnancy and it had me contemplating whether I would eventually tell him.

On many nights I would pray and pray, wishing and hoping the baby would somehow magically be his. Reality always settled in, and I knew it wasn't. When it finally came out things between Elijah and I worsened. Everything that we had overcome in the past such as him having a baby on me right after our daughter was born, to him catching me fucking his best friend in one of his other friend's driveway, to even the years we'd been together and I was soliciting myself to provide our family with the necessities we needed to survive, down to me losing my engagement ring at another nigga's house he was beefing with only to turn around and have a baby with another enemy couldn't have prepared me for those months of hell. Our relationship had always been dysfunctional even from the start, so it was best to just end it.

Closing that chapter left me wondering. I was messing with Austin and spending time with a man I met named "Dymond" who I had met previously. He had left me alone while I was going through this same situation with Austin and Elijah back before I had gotten pregnant. It was ironic because he left me alone because of that drama and entered back into my life when it had gotten worse. Now I had another baby while being stalked by Austin's new girlfriend, who was the little sister of his other baby mom. It had come out that he had been fucking that little girl since she was 12-years old when she would come to babysit for her sister. She turned around years later to have a baby with him too. I decided to finally let all that drama go and focus on my new friend.

Dymond was an entrepreneur who had multiple businesses. He inspired me to boss my life up. I was grateful that he came back into my life. I was still all over the place but before he left back out my life, he had completely bossed it all the way up.

True Love: AllInOne

Imagine waking up and you have a desire to change your life completely and undoubtedly. That was me. I had had enough of the bullshit that I'd succumbed my whole existence to. One day I just woke up and said I was tired of living my life like this. My life was unstructured, drama-filled, and depressing. I was tired of having sex with multiple men for money and always ending up alone. It wasn't worth it. None of it. I had to make a change.

I decided to do exactly what Dymond bred me to do, something that I didn't know was in me already. I started a program collecting clothing donations and giving them back out to families in need. When I became versed in that I moved and started a girls group getting young teenagers every Friday doing activities with them and giving them something to do to keep them out the streets. I ran both programs with my hard-earned money, sometimes even going broke, but I didn't care because I liked the change. I knew something new and great was in store for me.

It seemed like every time something good was going for me something, or someone, toxic resurfaced testing everything I had accomplished. Dymond and I were doing great. He had me accomplishing things I never imagined for myself. Around this time Sugar #1 popped back up. I can't lie and say that I didn't let him in because I did. This man had carried me through most of my teenage and adult years, but he was toxic. He feared that I would cut him off and leave him for good and reminded me every day of how he'd gotten me this far. What he didn't know was that my new man had done what no one that I'd ever experienced before had done and that was to help me find myself. He made me realize that the prize was me. Not my pussy, or how well I fucked, it was me and the woman inside me standing behind the scared little girl who was afraid to open the door and let her out.

Sugar #1 was the main reason that Elijah and I separated and eventually became the reason me and Dymond didn't last. I wouldn't say he was completely the reason because Dymond was a muthafucka too. Though he'd bossed me up and inspired me to change my life he'd spent many days tearing me down. He often made me feel like I wasn't good enough for him but by then it was too late. He had done everything to make me feel worthy that when he switched up, I switched him out. His manipulation didn't work on me because he taught me that.

Nearly a year after I decided to rid all the men that I allowed to hold me back and hinder me from being great I turned up. I started going hard for my companies, manifesting new business ventures that ultimately lead me to the love of my life. ALLinONE and "Easy" my new friend.

Easy was the photographer who did a photo shoot that I had booked to promote my business. At first sight, he wasn't anyone that I'd even take a second glance at. He wasn't the type of guy I would normally date, at least he didn't come off that way. I was judging a book by its cover. He dressed nice and talked properly. He carried himself with class. How did we end up dating? I still don't know. Though it wasn't love at first sight it had to be something because we weren't feeling each other on that level, but somehow, we fell for each other.

We started getting serious and I didn't want anything from my past to affect us like it had done other guys that I had expressed interest in before, in and between, my relations spoken about during this memoir. I pulled up on him and gave him all of Indigo Norwood, Indigo Blue better known as Mrs. Understood. I broke it all down to him about my past niggas I had been with and dated to me selling pussy all that. I explained to him my reasons then and how I had changed and was still changing and wanting to do better for myself.

We dated for a year and things started to get very serious between us. We moved in together and I quit the job I had maintained for 5-years and had decided to focus on my business full time. Things were rough the first year of me transitioning and I fell hard back into what I did best. I was older now and I knew a little more so instead of hiding it from Easy I let him in, and he helped me prostitute right and made sure I was safe. Selling pussy was what I knew for sure I was good at and knowing that Easy was okay with it I mastered it. Instead of selling myself short and having everyone in my city in my business, I started hitting licks out of town. He would always go with me, waiting outside, and we'd come back with bands. We made a promise that we would go in and come right out. We had promised each other that it was temporary for us to just stack some money, invest in our businesses, and when we finished, we would have a baby. We did just that.

It wasn't always easy, and we had run into a few life-or-death situations. One time we went, and a man had given me a fake address, which was an address for an empty restaurant and both of our intuitions told us to leave and just as we pulled off, we passed the S.W.A.T team headed in that same direction. Scared we backed off, but the money was too good and easy for it to be forever, and we leaped right back in when we felt the time was right. It was for a while and then we ran into another situation. I had booked a Superbowl party in Cleveland and we pulled up, bags packed ready to make that bread and the F.E.D.S were waiting for us to walk in, and to my surprise, I found out that they had been building a case on me. I had so many upscale clients, mostly white businessmen, they thought that they were hitting a big takedown, but I wasn't the scandal type.

After being followed for some time, they pulled us over but couldn't hold us because they didn't have enough to arrest us on. We made it home safe that night, but I was scared to death because I had come too far to get jammed up and had too much to lose, including my kids, and the future I was building for myself. We promised each other that night that we were done, and I wanted to be done but I was addicted to the power and money. So though Easy and I promised that we were out I went behind his back, sneaking and catching plays without telling him.

Why I did it? I still don't know. It was so easy at that time for me to convince him to do whatever I wanted. Maybe I just need that extra excitement.

Nonetheless, he found out because one of the times the condom had broken inside me. The tension between us was thick and he stopped trusting me. For a long time, we had problems and I was disgusted for wrecking something so good by doing something so dumb. However, we bounced back, and I promised myself and him that I'd never be disloyal again. Despite the pact we made to get out he allowed me to keep tricking, but only with my regulars.

One night we made our usual drive to Canton, Ohio for me to meet up with one of my regulars. He was a big payer and always paid top dollar. He was into kinky shit some examples are him tying me up in his basement naked, making me call him master while he called me a nigger. I mean some real kinky shit that I won't even go into detail about, but he always paid so I always complied.

On this particular night, his request made me throw in the towel and I vowed to never revert into my soliciting ways. After our hour-long sexcapade, we were getting cleaned up as we discussed our next meeting. He told me he wanted to change things up a bit and requested that our next meeting begin with him putting me into the trunk of his car and drive me to a restaurant. Bringing a cup of sperm, he wanted to watch as I ate it off a plate. He knew how strange and absurd his request was, but he was willing to pay top dollar, whatever I wanted, to allow him to do it. I wasn't comfortable with it just listening to it made me feel strange. His eyes were glossy, and he seemed to be in a trance as he gave step-by-step details of what he had in store for me, and it didn't sit right. I left that night never reaching out to him again nor anyone else. I told Easy about what he wanted, and he agreed that he was probably going to kill me and that put the icing on the cake. We were out of the game for good!

I'd be lying if I said that I never thought about it again or wondered what would've happened if I had gone through with his preposterous request and gotten into that trunk. I'm okay with never finding out and ever since that day we stuck by what we promised and never went back. We found a legit way to follow our dreams and for a long time after we counted the money and saved, we invested it into my businesses and purchased our first home together. Though life always throws curve balls we have since separated but I still am working and fighting for a better life for me and mine.

So, when you hear my name from this point on you know my story from my own mouth. You've read my words and dipped into my eternal existence. You now have a clear understanding of why I move the way I move and why I deal with certain people how I deal with them. When you mention my name make sure you provide the person, you're mentioning me to with a full, accurate, and complete definition of who I am.

I am Indigo Norwood, a young woman who was once broken, but now is placing the pieces back together.

I am Indigo Norwood, a survivor who is still haunted, still growing, using the discrepancies of the life she wanted, the life she feared, and the life she lived as the motivation she needs to live the life she deserves.

I am Mrs. Understood, a woman who has accepted and learned that everyone who judges aren't always able to and/or equipped to judge. I know that all my means to provide haven't always been good, but that's my motivation as a CEO.

I am a survivor of mental and physical abuse, a survivor of molestation and abandonment. I could have chosen a different path instead I chose to turn what I've been through into a positive and valuable investment. A financial investment and an investment into the life bank. I am resilient. I am Indigo Blue.

Something for YOU!

The following pages are for you! I have taken you through my journey of abandonment, depression, self-hate, and much more. One thing that helped me grow from the trauma was journaling. So, the next few pages are provided to get you to take the first step. Write. I would like you to write about goals, to clear your head, and heal from your own personal traumas. Take the time to journal and figure out your life's purpose or clarify what you already have planned. Write whatever you desire to help you start your next steps to overcoming trauma.

Your Best & Worst

I would like you to take the time out to reflect on some of your Best and Worst times in life.

Describe your best day:

_____

_____

Describe your worst day:

_____

_____

What was the best thing someone has ever said about you? How did that make you feel? Why do you think it had this impact?

_____

_____

_____

_____

What was the worst thing someone has ever said to you? How did that make you feel? Why do you think it had this impact on you?

_____

_____

_____

What are you best at? This can be at work, at school, at home, a feeling, anything:

_____

_____

_____

What are you the worst at? This can be at work, at school, at home, a feeling, anything:

_____

_____

_____

_____

In a few sentences, bullet points, dashes, however you want to answer, what is the best part of you? What is the best part of your mind? Body? Take a good look at yourself and talk about what is the best about you.

_____

_____

_____

_____

_____

_____

_____

_____

_____

_____

_____

In a few sentences, bullet points, dashes, however you want to answer, what is the worst part of you? What is the worst part of your mind? Body? Take a good look at yourself and talk about what is the worst about you.

___

___

___

___

___

___

___

___

___

___

Now that you have taken the time to reflect on what are the best and worst part of YOU, talk about how you are feeling now?

_____
_____
_____
_____
_____
_____
_____
_____
_____
_____
_____
_____

Changes

On the lines provided below, list 10 things in your life that you can't change. Then List 10 things that you can change. Take your time and think it through. Remember it's okay if you aren't able to fill in exactly 10!

I Can Change	I Can't Change

Just Write!

Take the next few pages to journal whatever you desire. I hope that it gives you the release that it has given me.

_____

_____

_____

_____

_____

_____

_____

_____

www.ingramcontent.com/pod-product-compliance
Lightning Source LLC
LaVergne TN
LVHW021600070426
835507LV00014B/1879